Mastering Digital Copywriting: Crafting Compelling Content for SEO, Email, and Social Media Success

Table of contents

INTRODUCTION

Welcome to "Mastering Digital Copywriting: Crafting Compelling Content for SEO, Email, and Social Media Success." In the vast landscape of digital marketing, the ability to wield words effectively is an invaluable skill. This ebook is your guide to mastering the art and science of persuasive copywriting tailored for the dynamic digital realm.

In today's digital age, where attention spans are fleeting and competition is relentless, compelling copy stands as the linchpin of successful marketing strategies. Whether it's capturing the essence of a brand, engaging an audience, or driving conversions, the words we use hold unparalleled influence.

This comprehensive guide is designed to equip you with the essential tools and strategies to elevate your copywriting prowess. We'll embark on a journey through the intricate nuances of crafting attention-grabbing headlines, infusing emotions into content, optimizing for search engines without compromising quality, and much more.

Throughout this ebook, we'll explore actionable techniques and real-world examples that bridge the gap between effective writing and digital marketing success. From unraveling the mysteries of SEO-driven content to mastering the art of captivating email subject lines and engaging social media copy, each chapter is crafted to empower you with practical knowledge and actionable insights.

Whether you're a seasoned marketer seeking to refine your skills or a novice venturing into the captivating world of digital copywriting, this ebook aims to be your trusted companion. Get ready to unleash the power of words and transform your digital marketing endeavors with compelling, results-driven copy.

Let's embark on this enriching journey together and unlock the potential of persuasive digital copywriting in the vibrant landscape of online marketing.

1. **Understanding Copywriting:**

a) **Introduction to Copywriting in Digital Marketing:**

Understanding copywriting involves grasping several key elements:

1. Understanding the Audience: Effective copy is tailored to resonate with a specific audience. To understand copywriting, start by understanding who you're writing for—their preferences, pain points, and motivations.

2. Clarity and Persuasion: Copywriting is about communicating a message clearly and persuasively. It involves structuring content in a way that captivates attention, maintains interest, builds desire, and encourages action (the AIDA model: Attention, Interest, Desire, Action).

3. Emotional Appeal: Copywriting often leverages emotions to connect with readers. Understanding how to evoke emotions like joy, fear, curiosity, or urgency can significantly impact the effectiveness of your writing.

4. Value Proposition: Effective copy clearly communicates the benefits and value of a product, service, or idea. Understanding how to highlight these aspects succinctly is crucial.

5. Call-to-Action (CTA): A CTA is a vital element of copywriting—it's the prompt that directs the reader to take a specific action. Understanding how to craft

compelling CTAs is a key aspect of mastering copywriting.

6. Adaptability and Continual Learning: Copywriting evolves with trends and audience behavior. It requires staying updated on best practices, testing new techniques, and being adaptable to changes in consumer preferences and platforms

b)   Importance and Impact of Effective Copy:

Captures Attention:

- First Impression: Effective copy immediately grabs the audience's attention. Compelling headlines, engaging opening lines, or intriguing subject lines in emails are critical in making a strong first impression.

- In a Sea of Content: In today's information-saturated world, good copy distinguishes itself, cutting through the noise to capture the audience amidst numerous distractions.

Drives Engagement:

- Creates Interest: Well-crafted copy maintains interest, keeping the audience engaged throughout the content.

- Encourages Interaction: Whether it's prompting likes, shares, comments, or clicks, effective copy encourages interaction and participation.

Influences Decisions:

- Guides Decision-Making: Persuasive copy influences consumer decisions by highlighting the benefits, solving problems, or creating desire for a product or service.

- Builds Trust and Credibility: Convincing and credible copy fosters trust, crucial for making informed decisions, especially in the digital space.

Boosts Conversions:

- Direct Impact on Sales: In marketing, the ultimate goal is often conversion—making a sale, gaining a subscriber, or securing a sign-up. Effective copy significantly increases conversion rates.

- Clear Call-to-Action (CTA): Direct and persuasive CTAs, a part of effective copy, guide users towards the desired action.

Shapes Brand Image:

- Reflects Brand Personality: The tone, style, and messaging in copywriting contribute to shaping a brand's identity and personality.

- Consistency and Cohesion: Consistent and well-aligned messaging across various platforms and campaigns reinforce brand identity.

Enhances SEO and Visibility:

- SEO-Friendly Content: Quality copy that incorporates relevant keywords and provides valuable information improves search engine rankings, driving organic traffic.

- Increased Visibility: Appearing in search results due to effective copy increases brand visibility and attracts potential customers.

Effective copywriting, therefore, serves as the backbone of successful marketing and communication strategies. It's a powerful tool that not only informs and engages but also influences and drives action, contributing significantly to the success and growth of businesses and brands.

c) **Basics of Persuasive Writing and Its Role in Marketing:**

Understanding the basics of persuasive writing is fundamental in crafting compelling marketing content. Here's a breakdown of its role and essential elements:

Role in Marketing:

1. Influence and Engagement: Persuasive writing aims to influence the audience's thoughts, emotions, and behaviors. In marketing, it's crucial for engaging potential customers, driving conversions, and building brand loyalty.

2. Conveying Benefits and Value: It focuses on highlighting the benefits and value of products or services, addressing pain points, and demonstrating how the offering meets the audience's needs or desires.

3. Establishing Credibility and Trust: Persuasive writing builds trust and credibility by presenting information in a

convincing, credible, and relatable manner, fostering a connection with the audience.

Essential Elements:

1. Understanding the Audience: Effective persuasive writing begins with understanding the audience's needs, preferences, and motivations. Tailoring the message to resonate with them is key.

2. Clear Communication: Clarity is crucial. Persuasive writing communicates the message clearly, avoiding ambiguity or confusion, ensuring the audience comprehends the information effortlessly.

3. Emotional Appeal: It often leverages emotions to connect with the audience on a deeper level. Appealing to emotions like joy, fear, desire, or empathy can influence decision-making.

4. Strong Argumentation: Presenting a compelling argument supported by evidence, facts, testimonials, or statistics reinforces the credibility of the message.

5. Action-Oriented Language: Persuasive writing includes strong, action-oriented language that encourages the audience to take a specific action, such as making a purchase, signing up, or sharing content.

6. Call-to-Action (CTA): A persuasive piece of writing often culminates in a clear and compelling CTA that prompts the audience to act.

Techniques in Persuasive Writing:

1. Rhetorical Devices: Employing techniques like repetition, analogies, or rhetorical questions to make the message more impactful.

2. Storytelling: Using narratives to evoke emotions and create a connection with the audience, making the content memorable and relatable.

3. Social Proof: Incorporating testimonials, reviews, or case studies to demonstrate the success or positive experiences of others.

4. Scarcity or Urgency: Creating a sense of scarcity or urgency to prompt immediate action, emphasizing limited offers or time-sensitive deals.

Understanding and mastering these elements of persuasive writing are essential for marketers to create content that resonates with their audience, drives engagement, and ultimately influences consumer behavior positively

2.   Crafting Compelling Headlines:

a) **Different Types of Headlines and Their Impact:**

Headlines play a crucial role in capturing attention and drawing readers into content. Understanding the various types of headlines and their impact helps in crafting compelling and engaging content. Here's an overview:

Different Types of Headlines:

1. **Informative Headlines:**

   - Purpose: Provides straightforward information about the content.

   - Impact: Direct and informative, these headlines quickly convey what the reader can expect from the content.

2. **How-To Headlines:**

   - Purpose: Offers guidance or instructions on achieving a particular goal.

   - Impact: Appeals to readers seeking solutions, promising actionable advice or steps to achieve a desired outcome.

3. **Question Headlines:**

   - Purpose: Engages readers by posing a question that triggers curiosity or addresses a common concern.

   - Impact: Invites readers to seek answers within the content, prompting them to continue reading for solutions or information.

4. **Listicle Headlines:**

- Purpose: Organizes content into a numbered list format, often providing tips, ideas, or insights.

- Impact: Easily scannable and enticing, listicle headlines promise specific information and are popular for their structured format.

5. **Shock or Controversial Headlines:**

- Purpose: Uses provocative or controversial language to grab attention.

- Impact: Generates curiosity or emotional response but should be used judiciously to avoid misleading or clickbait content.

6. **Curiosity/Ellipsis Headlines:**

- Purpose: Teases readers by creating an information gap or leaving an open question.

- Impact: Intrigues readers by hinting at something compelling but undisclosed, encouraging them to read further to satisfy their curiosity.

Impact of Different Headline Types:

- Attention-Grabbing: Each type of headline has its own way of capturing attention. Informative headlines are direct, while curiosity-driven or how-to headlines pique interest.

- Audience Engagement: Different types resonate differently with various audiences. For instance, listicles might appeal to those seeking concise information, while question headlines engage readers looking for answers.

- Content Structure: Headline types often determine the content structure. How-to headlines might introduce step-by-step guides, while listicle headlines organize content into numbered points.

Understanding these headline types and their impact helps content creators choose the most effective approach based on the content's nature, target audience, and objectives, ensuring that the headline serves as a compelling entry point to the content itself.

b) **Techniques for Writing Attention-Grabbing Headlines:**

Creating attention-grabbing headlines involves employing specific techniques that captivate readers and entice them to engage with the content. Here are several techniques to craft compelling headlines:

1. Use Power Words:

- Impactful Vocabulary: Incorporate strong and emotional words that evoke curiosity, urgency, or excitement, such as "essential," "unbelievable," or "transformative."

- Emotional Triggers: Words that evoke emotions, like "fear," "joy," or "surprise," can draw readers in by tapping into their feelings.

2. Pose Questions:

- Engage Curiosity: Use question headlines to prompt readers to seek answers or solutions within the content. Questions spark curiosity and encourage readers to find out more.

3. Create Curiosity or Tease:

- Information Gap: Hint at something intriguing but incomplete, leaving a gap that readers want to fill. This technique entices them to click to satisfy their curiosity.

- Teasing Content: Provide a glimpse of what's inside without revealing everything, compelling readers to explore further.

4. Offer Solutions or Benefits:

- Promise Value: Highlight the benefits or solutions that the content provides. Readers are attracted to headlines promising solutions to their problems or offering valuable insights.

5. Use Numbers and Lists:

- Quantify Information: Incorporate numbers into headlines to indicate specific tips, steps, or reasons, making the content more structured and enticing.

- Listicles: Frame the content as a list, as readers are often attracted to easily digestible and organized information.

6. Provoke Emotions or Intrigue:

- Emotional Appeal: Evoke emotions such as excitement, fear, or curiosity within the headline to evoke a response from readers.

- Intriguing Statements: Make bold or surprising statements that captivate attention and encourage readers to explore further.

7. Experiment with Length and Format:

- Short and Snappy: Concise headlines can be powerful, but longer, descriptive headlines might be necessary for more complex topics.

- Test Different Formats: Try different headline styles—questions, statements, or commands—to see what resonates best with your audience.

8. A/B Testing:

- Experiment and Analyze: Test different headline variations to gauge audience response. Analyze metrics to determine which headline style performs best and refine your approach accordingly.

By utilizing these techniques, writers can create headlines that not only grab attention but also compel readers to delve deeper into the content, ultimately increasing engagement and driving traffic.

c)   Examples and Exercises for Practice:

Here are examples and exercises to help you practice crafting attention-grabbing headlines:

Examples of Attention-Grabbing Headlines:

1. **Power Words:**

   - "Discover 10 Life-Changing Strategies for Ultimate Productivity!"

   - "Uncover the Secret to Effortless Weight Loss in 30 Days!"

2. **Question Headlines:**

   - "Are You Making These Common Financial Mistakes?"

   - "Want to Know the Best Travel Hacks for Budget Explorers?"

3. **Curiosity and Tease:**

   - "The Shocking Truth Behind Common Health Myths..."

- "This Simple Trick Can Save You Hours Every Day – Find Out How!"

4. **Offer Solutions or Benefits:**

   - "Unlock Your Potential: Master the Art of Persuasive Writing Today!"

   - "Boost Your Sales with Proven Marketing Strategies: Start Now!"

Exercises for Practicing Headline Writing:

1. **Topic-Based Practice:**

   - Choose a topic you're passionate about. Craft at least five different headlines using various techniques (power words, questions, curiosity, benefits, etc.) for that topic.

2. **A/B Testing:**

   - Create two versions of a headline for a piece of content you've written or plan to write. Test these headlines on a small audience (friends, colleagues, or online platforms) to see which one garners more interest or engagement.

3. **Headline Revisions:**

- Find existing headlines from articles, blog posts, or news stories. Rewrite these headlines using different techniques to make them more engaging or attention-grabbing.

4. **Timed Writing Practice:**

   - Set a timer for 10-15 minutes. Challenge yourself to generate as many headline variations as possible within the time limit for a specific topic or content idea.

5. **Feedback and Analysis:**

   - Share your crafted headlines with peers or writing groups. Gather feedback on which headlines they find most compelling and why. Use this feedback to refine your headline-writing skills.

6. **Real-time Testing:**

   - Use social media platforms to test different versions of headlines for the same content. Monitor engagement metrics (likes, shares, clicks) to determine which headline resonates most with your audience.

Practicing with these exercises and examples allows you to experiment with different headline-writing techniques, refine your skills, and gain a better understanding of what resonates most effectively with your audience.

3. Creating Persuasive Content:

a) The Power of Storytelling in Marketing:

The power of storytelling in marketing is immense—it's a compelling tool that allows brands to connect with their audience on a deeper, emotional level. Here's an exploration of the significance of storytelling in marketing:

Establishes Emotional Connection:

- Humanizes Brands: Stories create an emotional bond, making brands relatable and personable. They transcend features and benefits, allowing audiences to connect with the brand's values and ethos.

- Elicits Emotions: Well-crafted narratives evoke emotions, whether it's joy, empathy, nostalgia, or inspiration, prompting a more profound connection with the audience.

Enhances Brand Recall and Recognition:

- Memorability: Stories stick in our minds better than facts or figures. Memorable narratives make brands stand out, fostering better recall among consumers.

- Unique Identity: Compelling stories help carve a unique identity for a brand, differentiating it from competitors and resonating with consumers.

Engages and Captivates Audiences:

- Captivating Content: Stories captivate attention and maintain interest. They offer a compelling way to convey information, keeping audiences engaged and eager to learn more.

- Longer Attention Spans: Engrossing narratives hold attention for longer periods, ensuring a deeper engagement with the brand message.

Builds Trust and Loyalty:

- Establishes Trust: Stories build trust by showcasing authenticity and transparency. They allow brands to share their journey, values, and successes, fostering credibility among consumers.

- Creates Advocates: Compelling stories turn consumers into brand advocates, as they feel a personal connection and are more likely to share the brand's story with others.

Drives Action and Conversions:

- Influences Decision-Making: Stories have the power to influence consumer behavior. They inspire action by creating a desire for a product or service, ultimately driving conversions.

- Narrative CTAs: Well-integrated stories often lead to more effective calls-to-action (CTAs) by providing context and emotional resonance for the desired action.

Examples of Successful Storytelling in Marketing:

- Nike's "Just Do It" Campaign: Tells stories of determination and overcoming obstacles, inspiring consumers to push their limits.

- Apple's Product Launch Events: Utilizes storytelling to unveil new products, focusing on innovation, simplicity, and the human experience.

Implementation Strategies:

- Identify Brand Stories: Find narratives that align with the brand's values, heritage, or customer experiences.

- Use Multiple Platforms: Share stories across various platforms—social media, websites, videos—to reach a wider audience.

- Customer-Centric Approach: Highlight customer stories or testimonials to create a personal connection with the audience.

Storytelling in marketing isn't just about narratives; it's about creating meaningful connections, fostering brand loyalty, and inspiring action—a powerful tool in building lasting relationships with consumers.

b)   **Using Emotions and Relatability in Content Creation:**

Utilizing emotions and relatability in content creation is a potent strategy to connect deeply with audiences.

Here's an exploration of how emotions and relatability enhance content:

Evoking Emotions:

1. Establishes Connection: Emotions, such as joy, empathy, or nostalgia, create a human connection between the audience and the content, making it more memorable and impactful.

2. Drives Engagement: Emotionally resonant content triggers reactions and encourages sharing, leading to increased engagement and interaction among audiences.

3. Shapes Perception: Emotional content influences how audiences perceive a brand or message. Positive emotions associated with content can positively impact brand perception.

Leveraging Relatability:

1. Understanding Audience Needs: Relatable content addresses the audience's pain points, challenges, or aspirations, demonstrating an understanding of their experiences and needs.

2. Enhancing Engagement: Relatable content draws in the audience by making them feel understood, fostering a sense of belonging or identification.

3. Building Trust and Authenticity: Relatability in content creation helps in establishing trust and authenticity, showing that the brand understands and values its audience.

Strategies for Emotionally Relatable Content:

1. Tell Human-Centric Stories: Share stories that highlight real experiences, struggles, or successes. Authentic narratives resonate deeply with audiences.

2. Use Visuals and Imagery: Engaging visuals complement emotional content, amplifying the impact and evoking stronger emotional responses.

3. Empathy and Understanding: Show empathy towards audience challenges, and demonstrate an understanding of their situations.

4. Personalization and Tailoring: Craft content that feels personalized, addressing specific audience segments or individual needs.

Examples of Emotionally Relatable Content:

- Dove's "Real Beauty" Campaign: Embraces diversity and challenges beauty standards, resonating with women of all shapes, sizes, and backgrounds.

- Always' "Like a Girl" Campaign: Addresses stereotypes and empowers girls and women, striking an emotional chord.

Implementation in Content Creation:

- Audience Research: Understand the emotions and experiences your audience relates to and resonates with.

- Empathy-Driven Content: Create content that empathizes with your audience's challenges or aspirations, offering solutions or support.

- Consistency and Authenticity: Maintain authenticity and consistency in tone and messaging across all content to build trust and reliability.

By infusing content with emotions and relatability, brands can create deeper connections, foster stronger engagement, and establish enduring relationships with their audience.

c)   **Case Studies or Examples Demonstrating Successful Persuasive Content:**

Case studies and examples showcasing successful persuasive content illustrate how specific strategies and techniques have driven engagement, conversions, and brand success. Here are a few examples:

1. **Airbnb's "Experiences" Campaign:**

- Strategy: Airbnb leveraged persuasive storytelling to promote its "Experiences" feature.

- Execution: They highlighted real stories of hosts and guests, showcasing unique experiences that travelers could book.

- Impact: By focusing on personal narratives and emotional connections, Airbnb increased bookings and engagement, encouraging travelers to explore new destinations.

2. Coca-Cola's "Share a Coke" Campaign:

- Strategy: Coca-Cola personalized their product by printing people's names on their bottles.

- Execution: This approach created a sense of personalization and connection with consumers, encouraging them to find and share their names or special messages on social media.

- Impact: The campaign generated buzz, increased social media mentions, and enhanced consumer engagement, leading to boosted sales and brand loyalty.

3. Always' "#LikeAGirl" Campaign:

- Strategy: Always challenged societal norms by addressing stereotypes associated with doing things "like a girl."

- Execution: The campaign featured a powerful video highlighting the impact of the phrase "like a girl" on young girls' self-esteem.

- Impact: It sparked a global conversation, garnered millions of views, and empowered women and girls worldwide, aligning the brand with a powerful social cause and boosting brand perception.

4. HubSpot's Content Marketing:

- Strategy: HubSpot's content marketing focuses on educational, value-driven content, providing solutions to common marketing challenges.

- Execution: They offer free resources like guides, templates, and webinars to educate and assist their audience.

- Impact: By providing valuable content, HubSpot has established itself as a thought leader in the industry, attracting leads and converting them into customers.

5. Dollar Shave Club's Viral Video:

- Strategy: Dollar Shave Club created a humorous and engaging video showcasing their subscription service.

- Execution: The video was witty, addressing pain points associated with expensive razors and emphasizing convenience and affordability.

- Impact: The video went viral, attracting millions of views, driving subscriptions, and rapidly expanding their customer base.

These examples demonstrate the effectiveness of persuasive content strategies—from storytelling and personalization to challenging norms and providing value—

which resulted in increased brand awareness, engagement, and conversions. They showcase how understanding the audience and employing persuasive techniques can significantly impact a brand's success.

4.   SEO Copywriting:

a)   Basics of SEO and Its Connection to Copywriting:

Basics of SEO:

1. Keyword Research: Identifying relevant keywords and phrases that users search for in search engines. These keywords help in understanding user intent and crafting content around these queries.

2. On-Page Optimization: Optimizing content elements on the webpage, including titles, meta descriptions, headings, and URL structures, to align with targeted keywords and enhance visibility.

3. Quality Content Creation: Creating high-quality, informative, and engaging content that satisfies user intent, provides value, and aligns with search engine algorithms.

4. Link Building: Acquiring high-quality backlinks from reputable websites, as they serve as 'votes of confidence' for search engines, indicating the content's credibility and authority.

5. Technical SEO: Addressing technical aspects like website speed, mobile-friendliness, site architecture, and structured data to enhance user experience and search engine crawl ability.

Connection to Copywriting:

1. Keyword Integration: Copywriting involves seamlessly integrating relevant keywords into content without compromising readability or quality. Keywords should naturally fit within the content to optimize for search engines.

2. Content Structure and Formatting: Well-structured content with clear headings, subheadings, and proper formatting not only enhances readability but also aids search engine crawlers in understanding the content's context.

3. User-Centric Approach: Copywriting for SEO involves prioritizing the audience's needs while incorporating targeted keywords. It focuses on creating content that answers queries and provides value to users.

4. Meta Tags and Descriptions: Crafting compelling meta titles and descriptions using targeted keywords to attract clicks from search engine results pages (SERPs).

5. Linkable and Shareable Content: Writing content that is informative, unique, and valuable encourages organic linking from other websites and social shares, contributing to SEO performance.

Best Practices for SEO Copywriting:

1. Research and Use of Keywords: Utilize keyword research tools to identify relevant keywords and strategically incorporate them into the content.

2. Content Optimization: Ensure the content addresses user queries effectively while maintaining readability and relevance.

3. Unique and Engaging Content: Create original, valuable, and engaging content that stands out from competitors and encourages user interaction.

4. Regularly Update Content: Periodically update and refresh content to keep it relevant and aligned with current search trends.

5. Monitor and Analyze Performance: Track content performance using analytics tools, making data-driven decisions to refine strategies and improve results.

b)   Keyword Research Methods and Tools:

Methods for Keyword Research:

1. **Brainstorming and Seed Keywords:**

   - Start with broad topics related to your content or industry.

   - Use seed keywords (main terms) and expand on them to find related phrases.

2. **Google Autocomplete and Related Searches:**

- Utilize Google's autocomplete feature to find variations of search queries as you type in the search bar.

- Scroll down to the bottom of the search results page to find related searches.

3. **Competitor Analysis:**

- Analyze competitors' websites to identify keywords they are ranking for.

- Use tools to explore their top-performing keywords and content strategies.

4. **Use of Online Tools:**

- Employ keyword research tools such as Google Keyword Planner, SEMrush, Ahrefs, Moz Keyword Explorer, Ubersuggest, and AnswerThePublic.

- These tools provide insights into keyword search volumes, competition, related terms, and trends.

Tools for Keyword Research:

1. **Google Keyword Planner:**

- Offers insights into search volumes, competition levels, and keyword suggestions based on your input.

2. **SEMrush:**

- Provides comprehensive keyword analytics, competitor analysis, and related keyword suggestions.

3. **Ahrefs:**

    - Offers keyword research tools, backlink analysis, and competitive data to aid in content strategy.

4. **Moz Keyword Explorer:**

    - Helps find relevant keywords, assess their difficulty, and discover SERP features.

5. **Ubersuggest:**

    - Offers keyword ideas, search volume data, and content suggestions based on keywords.

6. **AnswerThePublic:**

    - Generates content ideas by visualizing search queries as questions or prepositions.

Steps for Effective Keyword Research:

1. **Define Your Goals and Audience:**

    - Understand your target audience's interests, pain points, and search behavior.

    - Align keywords with the content you want to create and the audience you want to reach.

2. **Generate Keyword Ideas:**

    - Use a mix of methods and tools to collect a wide range of potential keywords related to your niche.

3. **Analyze and Refine:**

- Evaluate keyword metrics like search volume, competition, and relevance to prioritize and filter your keyword list.

4. **Consider Long-Tail Keywords:**

   - Include long-tail keywords (more specific, longer phrases) that target niche or specific audience queries.

5. **Regularly Review and Update:**

   - Keyword trends evolve; regularly review and update your keyword strategy to stay relevant.

c) **Strategies for Incorporating Keywords Effectively into Content:**

Keyword Placement:

- Title and Headings: Include keywords naturally in the title and subheadings to signal the content's relevance.

- Introductory Paragraph: Incorporate the main keyword early in the content's introduction to establish context.

- Body Content: Sprinkle keywords naturally throughout the content, ensuring they fit contextually without overstuffing.

2. Prioritize User Intent and Readability:

- Focus on Content Value: Write for the audience first, addressing their needs and interests while naturally incorporating keywords.

- Maintain Readability: Avoid keyword stuffing; use variations, synonyms, and natural language to maintain readability.

3. Use Keywords in Visual and Multimedia Elements:

- Image Alt Text: Optimize image alt text with relevant keywords to improve accessibility and assist search engine indexing.

- Video Titles and Descriptions: Incorporate keywords into video titles, descriptions, and transcripts for better search visibility.

4. Employ Internal and External Linking:

- Internal Links: Link relevant content within your website using anchor text that includes keywords, aiding in content discoverability and site navigation.

- External Links: Link to credible external sources using keywords where appropriate, enhancing content credibility.

5. Optimize Meta Tags and Descriptions:

- Meta Title and Description: Craft meta titles and descriptions that include keywords and compel users to click, enhancing SERP visibility.

6. Monitor Keyword Density and Placement:

- Natural Usage: Aim for a natural keyword distribution without forcefully inserting keywords; focus on making content coherent and valuable.

- Keyword Density: Maintain a balanced keyword density (around 1-2%) to avoid over-optimization.

7. Update and Refresh Content:

- Periodic Review: Regularly review and update content to reflect current trends, updating keywords if necessary.

8. Use Tools for Validation and Optimization:

- SEO Plugins and Tools: Utilize SEO tools and plugins (like Yoast SEO or SEMrush) to validate keyword usage and optimize content for better performance.

9. Test and Refine:

- A/B Testing: Experiment with different keyword variations and placement strategies to identify what works best for your audience and content.

10. Contextual Relevance:

- Focus on Topic Relevance: Ensure that keywords used align contextually with the overall theme and topic of the content.

5.   Email Marketing Copy:

a)   Importance of Subject Lines in Email Marketing:

1. First Point of Contact:

Initial Attention Grabber: Subject lines are the first thing recipients see. They determine whether an email captures attention among numerous others in the inbox.

Decision-Making Factor: The decision to open an email is often influenced by the subject line's appeal and relevance.

2. Increases Open Rates:

Key Driver of Open Rates: A compelling subject line directly impacts open rates. Intriguing or personalized subject lines entice recipients to open the email.

A/B Testing: Testing different subject lines allows marketers to identify which ones resonate best with their audience, ultimately improving open rates.

3. Sets Expectations and Intrigue:

Clarity and Intrigue: Well-crafted subject lines provide a clear idea of the email's content while leaving room for curiosity.

Communicates Value: They communicate the email's value proposition, prompting recipients to anticipate valuable information or offers.

4. Contributes to Engagement and Conversions:

Direct Engagement: Engaging subject lines encourage recipients to interact with the email, leading to higher click-through rates.

Influences Action: A persuasive subject line can influence recipients to take the desired action, such as making a purchase, signing up, or clicking a link.

5. Builds Brand Recognition and Trust:

Consistency and Branding: Establishing a consistent tone or style in subject lines reinforces brand identity and builds trust over time.

Quality Assurance: Effective subject lines align with the promised content, ensuring recipients associate the brand with valuable and relevant information.

6. Mobile Responsiveness:

Mobile Optimization: Given the prevalence of mobile usage, concise and attention-grabbing subject lines are essential for mobile users who often scan emails quickly.

7. Compliance and Deliverability:

Avoiding Spam Filters: Properly crafted subject lines help emails bypass spam filters by avoiding trigger words or misleading content that might flag them as spam.

Enhanced Deliverability: Relevant and engaging subject lines contribute to better email deliverability by encouraging recipients to interact with the email.

Strategies for Effective Subject Lines:

Personalization: Use recipient's names or tailored content based on preferences.

Urgency or Scarcity: Create a sense of urgency or limited availability to prompt immediate action.

Clarity and Relevance: Clearly communicate the email's content while aligning with recipients' interests.

Length and Formatting: Keep subject lines concise, mobile-friendly, and avoid spam-triggering words.

Testing and Optimization: Regularly test different subject lines to identify what resonates best with your audience.

b)   Writing Engaging Email Content and Personalization:

1. Understand Your Audience:

Segmentation: Divide your email list into segments based on demographics, behavior, or preferences.

Data Analysis: Use insights from past interactions to understand what content resonates best with different segments.

2. Personalization:

Customize Content: Tailor emails based on recipient data, such as their name, location, past purchases, or browsing behavior.

Dynamic Content: Use dynamic fields to populate specific information unique to each recipient, creating a personalized experience.

3. Compelling Subject Lines and Preheaders:

Engaging Openers: Craft subject lines that capture attention, evoke curiosity, and hint at the email's content.

Preheaders: Utilize preheader text effectively to complement subject lines and encourage opens.

4. Storytelling and Relevance:

Narrative Approach: Incorporate storytelling techniques to make the content relatable and engaging.

Relevant Content: Ensure emails provide valuable and relevant information, solving problems or addressing needs identified within your audience segments.

5. Clear and Compelling Copy:

Concise and Scannable: Use short paragraphs, bullet points, and headers for easy readability.

Strong Call-to-Actions (CTAs): Include clear, action-oriented CTAs that prompt recipients to take the desired action.

6. Visual Appeal:

Eye-Catching Design: Incorporate visually appealing elements such as images, GIFs, or videos that complement the content.

Responsive Design: Ensure emails are mobile-friendly for an optimal viewing experience across devices.

7. Interactive Content:

Surveys or Polls: Encourage engagement by including interactive elements like surveys or polls.

Quizzes or Contests: Incorporate fun and interactive elements that encourage participation.

8. Test and Iterate:

A/B Testing: Experiment with different elements like subject lines, content, CTAs, and personalization to gauge what resonates best with your audience.

Analytics Review: Analyze email performance metrics to understand which content drives engagement and conversions.

9. Timely and Relevant Messaging:

Triggered Emails: Send automated emails triggered by specific actions or events, providing timely and relevant information.

Seasonal Relevance: Tailor content to current events, holidays, or seasonal trends to enhance relevance.

10. Follow-Up and Relationship Building:

Post-Send Engagement: Engage with recipients who interact with your emails through follow-up content or offers.

Consistent Communication: Maintain a consistent schedule for sending emails, nurturing relationships over time.

c) **Crafting Effective CTAs for Emails:**

Crafting effective Call-to-Actions (CTAs) within emails is crucial for encouraging recipients to take desired actions. Here are strategies for creating compelling CTAs:

1. Clarity and Action-Oriented Language:

Clear and Specific: Use concise language that clearly communicates the action you want recipients to take.

Action-Oriented Verbs: Use verbs that prompt immediate action, such as "Shop Now," "Learn More," "Subscribe," "Get Started," etc.

2. Placement and Visibility:

Above the Fold: Position CTAs prominently, ideally near the top of the email and visible without scrolling.

Contrasting Colors: Use colors that make the CTA stand out and contrast with the email's background, attracting attention.

3. Personalization and Relevance:

Tailored Messaging: Personalize CTAs based on recipient behavior, preferences, or their position in the sales funnel.

Relevant to Content: Ensure the CTA aligns with the email's content and offers a logical next step for the recipient.

4. Create a Sense of Urgency or Scarcity:

Limited Time Offers: Use phrases like "Limited Time Offer" or "Ending Soon" to create urgency.

Scarcity Indicators: Highlight limited quantities or availability to encourage immediate action.

5. Benefit-Oriented:

Highlight Value Proposition: Clearly communicate the benefit or value recipients will gain by clicking the CTA.

Address Pain Points: Show how clicking the CTA can solve a problem or fulfill a need for the recipient.

6. Test Different Variations:

A/B Testing: Experiment with different CTA copy, colors, sizes, and placements to identify the most effective version.

Performance Analysis: Analyze metrics to determine which CTAs drive higher click-through rates and conversions.

7. Mobile Optimization:

Responsive Design: Ensure CTAs are easily clickable and prominently displayed on mobile devices to cater to mobile users.

Optimized Size: Make sure the CTA button is large enough for easy tapping on smaller screens.

8. Engaging Visuals:

Use of Icons or Buttons: Incorporate visually appealing buttons or icons to draw attention to the CTA.

Eye-Catching Design: Create visually compelling CTAs that complement the overall email design.

9. Testimonials or Social Proof:

Include Social Proof: Incorporate testimonials, reviews, or statistics that support the CTA to build credibility and trust.

10. Follow-Up and Reinforcement:

Post-Click Experience: Ensure the landing page after clicking the CTA aligns with the promise made in the email, maintaining a consistent user experience.

6. **Social Media Copywriting:**

a) **Tailoring Content for Different Platforms:**

1. **Understand Platform Dynamics:**

Audience Demographics: Know the demographics and behaviors of each platform's users.

Content Formats: Understand the types of content that perform best on each platform (images, videos, text, etc.).

Tone and Style: Adapt the tone, language, and style to match the platform's culture and communication norms.

2. **Customize Content for Each Platform:**

Visual Focus on Instagram and Pinterest: Emphasize high-quality visuals on image-centric platforms like Instagram and Pinterest. Use captivating images, infographics, or visually appealing content.

Conciseness on Twitter: Craft concise and engaging messages due to character limits on Twitter. Use hashtags strategically to increase visibility.

Professional and In-Depth on LinkedIn: Share industry insights, professional articles, or in-depth content suitable for a business-oriented audience.

Interactive and Visual on TikTok: Create short, engaging, and visually appealing videos that align with TikTok's trends and formats.

Engaging Stories on Snapchat: Utilize Stories format for time-sensitive, interactive, and engaging content on Snapchat.

3.   **Repurpose Content Across Platforms:**

Adaptation and Optimization: Repurpose content to fit the nuances of each platform. For instance, a blog post can become a series of tweets, an infographic, or a short video.

Maintain Consistent Branding: While adapting content, ensure consistent branding elements to maintain brand identity across platforms.

4.   **Use Platform-Specific Features:**

Utilize Features: Take advantage of unique features like Instagram Reels, Facebook Live, LinkedIn polls, etc., to engage with audiences in platform-specific ways.

Optimize for Algorithms: Understand and optimize content for each platform's algorithms to increase visibility and reach.

5.   **Tailor Content for User Behavior:**

Timing and Frequency: Post content at optimal times and adjust posting frequency based on platform-specific user behavior patterns.

Engagement and Interaction: Encourage engagement by responding to comments, participating in discussions, and leveraging platform-specific interactive features.

6.   **Measure and Adapt:**

Analytics and Insights: Use platform analytics to monitor content performance. Analyze what works best on each platform and adapt strategies accordingly.

b)   **Leveraging Visuals, Hashtags, and Character Limits:**

1.   **Visual Content:**

Importance of Visuals: Visuals, such as images, videos, infographics, and GIFs, capture attention more effectively than text alone.

Quality Matters: Use high-quality and visually appealing content to stand out in crowded feeds.

Consistent Branding: Maintain consistency in visual style, colors, and themes to reinforce brand identity across platforms.

Storytelling through Visuals: Use visuals to convey stories, evoke emotions, and communicate messages without relying solely on text.

2.   **Hashtags:**

Purpose of Hashtags: Help categorize content, increase discoverability, and reach a broader audience.

Relevant and Specific: Use relevant and specific hashtags that resonate with your content and target audience.

Research and Diversity: Research trending and industry-specific hashtags. Combine popular, niche, and branded hashtags for a balanced approach.

Limit Usage: Avoid overloading posts with hashtags; use a moderate number to maintain readability and effectiveness.

3.   **Character Limits:**

Platform Consideration: Platforms like Twitter have character limits, encouraging concise and impactful messages.

Crafting Concise Content: Focus on clarity and brevity. Communicate your message effectively within the character limit.

Use of Multimedia: Use images, videos, or links to convey additional information beyond text within character constraints.

Teasers and Call-to-Actions: Utilize character limits to create teasers or intriguing snippets that encourage users to engage or explore more.

4. **Best Practices:**

Visual-Hashtag Synergy: Combine visuals with relevant hashtags to amplify content reach and engagement.

Platform-Specific Optimization: Tailor content and use of hashtags based on each platform's norms, character limits, and audience behavior.

Testing and Optimization: Experiment with different combinations of visuals, hashtags, and concise text to identify what resonates best with your audience.

Engagement and Monitoring: Engage with users who interact with your content and monitor hashtag performance to refine your approach.

5. **Analytics and Adaptation:**

Track Performance: Use analytics tools to measure the impact of visuals and hashtags on engagement metrics like reach, likes, shares, and clicks.

Iterate and Improve: Based on analytics insights, adjust your visual content strategy and hashtag usage to optimize performance over time.

7.   Call-to-Action (CTA) Optimization:

Optimizing Call-to-Actions (CTAs) is crucial to prompt desired actions from your audience. Here's a comprehensive guide on CTA optimization:

1.   Clear and Action-Oriented Copy:

Clarity: Ensure the CTA's purpose is crystal clear. Use concise and direct language to convey the action you want users to take.

Action-Oriented Verbs: Use compelling verbs that inspire action, such as "Get," "Download," "Subscribe," "Shop," etc.

2.   Placement and Visibility:

Above the Fold: Position CTAs prominently, preferably near the top of the page or email where users can see it without scrolling.

Contrasting Colors: Use colors that make the CTA stand out against the background, attracting attention.

3.   Personalization and Relevance:

Tailored Messaging: Personalize CTAs based on user behavior, preferences, or demographics for increased relevance.

Content Alignment: Ensure the CTA aligns with the content users are engaging with, providing a logical next step.

4. **Create a Sense of Urgency or Scarcity:**

Limited-Time Offers: Use phrases like "Limited Time Only" or "Ending Soon" to create urgency.

Scarcity Indicators: Highlight limited quantities or availability to prompt immediate action.

5. **Design and Visual Elements:**

Button Design: Use visually appealing buttons that are easy to spot and click.

Iconography: Incorporate relevant icons or graphics to complement the CTA and draw attention.

6. **Mobile Optimization:**

Responsive Design: Ensure CTAs are mobile-friendly and easily clickable on different devices.

Size and Placement: Make CTAs large enough and well-positioned for comfortable tapping on mobile screens.

7. **A/B Testing and Iteration:**

Testing Variations: Experiment with different CTA copy, colors, sizes, and placements to determine the most effective version.

Performance Analysis: Analyze metrics to understand which CTAs drive higher click-through rates and conversions.

8.   **Personalize Based on User Journey:**

Stage-Specific CTAs: Tailor CTAs to different stages of the customer journey. Use awareness, consideration, and decision-based CTAs accordingly.

9.   **Value Proposition and Benefits:**

Highlight Benefits: Clearly communicate the value users will get by clicking the CTA, addressing their pain points or needs.

FOMO (Fear of Missing Out): Use persuasive language to emphasize what users might miss if they don't take action.

10.   **Follow-Up and Consistency:**

Consistent Experience: Ensure that the post-click experience matches the CTA promise, providing a seamless user journey.

11.   **Analytics and Iteration:**

Performance Tracking: Monitor CTA performance using analytics tools. Analyze data to refine strategies and optimize CTAs over time.

Conclusion:

In the realm of digital marketing, copywriting holds immense significance as it acts as the voice that communicates a brand's message to its audience. Crafting compelling and strategic content is pivotal in engaging and influencing consumers in the digital landscape.

Digital copywriting is not merely about words; it's about understanding the audience, their needs, behaviors, and the platforms they engage with. It involves storytelling, persuasion, and optimization techniques to drive desired actions.

A successful digital copywriter understands the power of persuasive language, the impact of SEO optimization, the art of storytelling, and the relevance of tailored content for different platforms. It's about creating content that not only captivates but also converts.

Moreover, the landscape of digital marketing and copywriting is ever-evolving. Strategies must adapt to technological advancements, changes in consumer behavior, and the emergence of new platforms and algorithms. Testing, analytics, and a commitment to continuous improvement are key in this dynamic environment.

Ultimately, the art of copywriting in digital marketing lies in striking a balance between creativity and data-driven strategies. It's about conveying brand messages in a way that resonates deeply with the audience, fosters engagement, drives conversions, and builds long-lasting relationships in the digital sphere.